IT'S TIME TO BAKE CHOCOLATE PEANUT BUTTER CUP COOKIES

It's Time to Bake CHOCOLATE PEANUT BUTTER CUP COOKIES

Walter the Educator

Silent King Books
A WhichHead Entertainment Imprint

Copyright © 2025 by Walter the Educator

All rights reserved. No part of this book may be reproduced in any manner whatsoever without written per- mission except in the case of brief quotations embodied in critical articles and reviews.

First Printing, 2025

Disclaimer

This book is a literary work; the story is not about specific persons, locations, situations, and/or circumstances unless mentioned in a historical context. Any resemblance to real persons, locations, situations, and/or circumstances is coincidental. This book is for entertainment and informational purposes only. The author and publisher offer this information without warranties expressed or implied. No matter the grounds, neither the author nor the publisher will be accountable for any losses, injuries, or other damages caused by the reader's use of this book. The use of this book acknowledges an understanding and acceptance of this disclaimer.

It's Time to Bake CHOCOLATE PEANUT BUTTER CUP COOKIES is a collectible early learning book by Walter the Educator suitable for all ages belonging to Walter the Educator's Time to Bake Book Series. Collect more books at WaltertheEducator.com

USE THE EXTRA SPACE TO TAKE NOTES AND DOCUMENT YOUR MEMORIES

CHOCOLATE PEANUT BUTTER CUP COOKIES

The sun is shining or snow may fall,

It's Time to Bake
Chocolate Peanut Butter Cup Cookies

It's time to bake, let's gather it all!

Chocolate and peanut butter in a yummy mix,

Cookies today? Let's make them quick!

Flour and sugar, soft and fine,

We scoop and measure, everything's in line.

In a big, round bowl, we'll stir with care,

Peanut butter cups? Oh, they'll go in there!

Butter so creamy, soft and sweet,

We mix it in, it's such a treat!

With eggs and vanilla, it's smooth as can be,

This dough is as perfect as dough should be!

The chocolate chips now tumble in,

A sprinkle of fun, it makes us grin.

And don't forget the peanut butter cups,

Chop them small, then toss them up!

It's Time to Bake Chocolate Peanut Butter Cup Cookies

Now roll the dough into little balls,

Round and ready, no matter how small.

Onto the tray, one by one,

This baking adventure is so much fun!

The oven's warm, the cookies will bake,

We wait and wiggle, it's hard to wait!

The smell of chocolate fills the air,

Soon we'll taste the love we've shared.

Ding! The timer says they're done,

It's Time to Bake Chocolate Peanut Butter Cup Cookies

Golden brown and smelling like fun.

Careful now, they're hot to touch,

But oh, they look so good, thank you so much!

We let them cool, it's hard to stay still,

The cookies sit on the windowsill.

Warm and chewy, gooey delight,

Chocolate peanut butter, what a sight!

It's time to taste, oh, what a bite!

Sweet and salty, the flavors unite.

A cookie so perfect, so yummy and round,

The best little treat we've ever found.

Now let's share with family and friends,

A cookie love that never ends.

Chocolate peanut butter, in every bite,

It's Time to Bake
Chocolate Peanut Butter Cup Cookies

Baking cookies makes everything right!

ABOUT THE CREATOR

Walter the Educator is one of the pseudonyms for Walter Anderson. Formally educated in Chemistry, Business, and Education, he is an educator, an author, a diverse entrepreneur, and he is the son of a disabled war veteran. "Walter the Educator" shares his time between educating and creating. He holds interests and owns several creative projects that entertain, enlighten, enhance, and educate, hoping to inspire and motivate you. Follow, find new works, and stay up to date with Walter the Educator™

at WaltertheEducator.com

www.ingramcontent.com/pod-product-compliance
Lightning Source LLC
LaVergne TN
LVHW052010060526
838201LV00059B/3945